The Chemists Key

Henry Nollius

CONTENTS

TheChemistsK eytoShutandOp   en:AstheT rueD octrineof theCor ruptionandGener ationinT enBriefAphorisms, IllustratedwithmostplainandfaithfulCommentaries,outof thePur eLightofNatur e:BythatJudiciousandIndustrious Artist

HenryNollius

1617

ToTheReader

This book having worth enough in itself needs not my commendation, this Author in his lifetime being an eminent physician and most able Philosopher as the discourse itself can best testify.

The translator also wanted not judgment to choose what was best in his kind, nor abilities to perform, the choice being made. It is I alone that appear here as Menelaus at that feast in the Iliad, who came though not invited. I shall not endeavor to excuse myself, for I come not empty but will contribute somewhat to the collation.

The Author builds on good principles, so that his Theory is as true as it is plausible; and I presume he aimed at nothing more, leaving all particulars and their application to the industry of his readers. He is sometimes pleased to descend to examples, but to such only as are natural, and they indeed are good to teach but hard to imitate. We see not all that Nature does.

When he speaks of rain and dew I am contented to think, he means something else than what is vulgarly so called. And I doubt not but his Salt petri is something different from that which is combustible and common. The Philosophers Dew, if I know it at all is a dry water, and their salt-peter is a most white incombustible body of a gummy aerial nature, and indeed, if my eyes have not deceived me, it is so aerial and unctuous that it will no more mingle with water than common oil will. I have for trial taken it in its gross body, and putting it in distilled rain water have digested it for a full fortnight, without the addition of any third thing, but they would never mix, the Nitre notwithstanding many long and violent agitations of the glass, keeping still apart in the form of butter or oil more white than snow. The truth is there is no affinity between this Salt-peter and water, for it is not made of water, but of air hid and condensed in water. We see also that the air is a dry spirit and wets nothing; but the mist or vapor of the water incorporating with the air wets all things. Even so those bodies or substances which are generated of air retain the first complexion of their parents; this dry aerial humidity being predominant in them as is evident in common quicksilver and in all resinous substances, as vegetable and mineral gums which will not mix with water. But this will not be more apparent to those who know that universal gum or sperm whereof Nitre is made, which is neither Dew nor Rain, but a water and no water; that is it is a dry water whereof see D'Espagnet in the 49 the canon of his first aphoristical part. Here is the reason then why Nitre Philosophical will not dissolve in nor mix with common water; for it is a fat, oleous, airy substance, made by natural congelation of a mercurial dry humidity which separates from phlegm, as is evident in that succus vitalis and great Lunary of Lully.

Nitre then or Mercury Philosophical is to be found in 150 places, and of several complexions.

In the great Hali Cali of Nature it is congealed and in a manner crucified between two extremes, and both of them venomous and caustic. If you know how to extract it thence in the form of buter or a most white sweet oil, then the ***, whence the Art has its name, is in your power, and D'Espagnet in his 225 canon will tell you what you have attained to.

Thus you see where the air of radical humidity is congealed; and now I must instruct you where it is a volatile and not congealed. It is so in the sperm whereof Nature immediately makes the Hali Cali, to which purpose the former author has left us a considerable maxim in his 214 canon: Rerum seminitz plurimus humidi radicalis inest; for this volatile air, which is in the seed or sperm reincrudates the fixed air which is in the Hali Cali. I say this volatile spermatic air or oil does it, and not oil of soap or salad, as some fools have dreamed; for nothing reincrudates and naturally dissolves a body but that crude sperm whereof the body was made. Most excellent in this respect is that passage in Lully Chap. XLVIII of his great testament: Quando volumes, quod siccum convertatur in humidii, cafrimus intrumuntum quod iesin aqua, quoequidus participal de humido radicali, viz. in vapore spiritus Quinta delatus est, etc. (When we wish to convert a dry thing into a moist thing, we take an agent which is in water --- one which partakes of the humid radical --- or rather in the vapor of aerial humidity disassociating it from its watery phlegm, in which the male spirit is carried). Thus Lully and now I think I have sufficiently introduced you; but if this be not enough I am afraid the whole discourse will not satisfy. I should have said much more, but that I intend shortly to publish a discourse of my own wherein I have endeavored to give some reasons for a most excellent and mysterious experience I have lately seen.

Eugenius Philalethes

TheAuthorsEpistle

Dedicatory to his noble friend and kinsman, the Lord Wygand Heymel,Pr esidentofDr esden,etc.

It is no long time (my honored Lord and patron) since there came to Gueilberg in quest of me, a most learned man, a professor of Logic and a Tutor of under-graduates in a certain famous University, who did earnestly entreat me to discover unto him those principles by which he might be introduced into the true knowledge of our most secret philosophy, finding him therefore to be a person of Singular Humanity, of most excellent abilities, and (as I perceived by frequent discourse) of a most acute and discerning apprehension, I resolved to grant his request; and for that end I did purposely lead him into a dissertation or reasoning about the Generation of natural bodies, and having brought him thither I advised him to search curiously after what manner, and by what means, this great and secret, though daily, work was performed: Signifying farther unto him, that the Foundation of our Art did, next to the divine assistance, consist chiefly in the perfect knowledge of Corruption and Generation. Now, though this answer and advice of mine did nothing like this learned man, seeming in this Book-judgment to be very simple and wise; nevertheless, that which I told him is the very truth; for he that perfectly knows the ways of Generation, will easily come to be acquainted with the true menstruum of every body, which in our philosophy is the most useful and difficult matter to come by; yea, he will find out a way or Process; which if he, by a right Imitation of Nature will wisely practice, he shall out of a convenient body (dissolved first, and digested in its own most natural and proper

Vinegar) perfectly extracted and attain to a most noble and precious medicine: A medicine I say, and not Gold; for the sophisters or Pseudo-Chymists, pining with an insatiable hunger after Gold, do by most covetous, chargeable and fruitless processes, infuse into their silly readers a strong desire of Gold-making, and promise them golden mountains; but Art cannot make Gold, Nature only produces substances; but how to perfect and purify imperfect metals by Nature only, and a natural way (not by adding to them, or mixing with them any extraneous substance or ingredient)and to separate and purge from them those obstructing, discordant impurities, which are the cause of their imperfection, the Philosophers do know very well.

Art, I say, cannot produce or make any substance; but how to propagate and multiply natures in their own species by transplantation and incision, he does know, but not without Nature. This I am sure of by the Light of Nature, whose only contemplation, with Gods blessing and gracious assistance has enabled me to write this short discourse of Generation, and wholly persuaded me to believe, that the sovereign true medicine must be sought and prepared, ad modum Generationis, after the same method that natural generations are performed.

Everything that nature affords for the subsistence and health of man its crude, and needs a further digestion, before it can be converted either into the substance of Man, or into a wholesome medicine: Let us consider our daily food; this grows in our gardens, is fed in our houses, and sown in our fields; but it is not turned into a blood and nutriment, before it is (after the Manner of Generation) altered, putrefied, and dissolved in our stomachs: That from this mass, so dissolved within us, the natural spirit may be extracted and communicated to the heart and the other members, for their conservation and strength, and so after other various digestions, the blood may become Seed, and turn into that radical Balsom, by whose virtue Mankind is both preserved and propagated: What hinders them, seeing out internal vessel of putrefaction is insufficient, but we may after the same manner, by natural means and a philosophic skill, so imitate and assist Nature, that all crude bodies whatsoever, may externally (without the Officina Ciborum) be set to putrefy, to be digested and dissolved until their spiritual nature may (after that solution) be easily extracted or taken out of them; by which spirit so extracted, our internal, vital spirit (for the singular Harmony that is betwixt them) would be so marvelously comforted and strengthened, that by this excellent kind of assistance, it would be brought to exercise all its faculties with such effectual activity and virtue, as would quickly expel and exterminate all the enemies and disturbers of life; I mean all diseases, though never so desperate.

If we certainly knew what that is what purifies all Seeds, and how it is done, without doubt we might and would by a constant industry (God assisting us) find out and prepare medicines truly philosophical, to the great advantage and comfort of Mankind. To this purpose Chymistry serves; for by the help of this Art we know how to digest, to dissolve, to putrefy to separate the impure from the pure, and so come by most perfect medicines: And verily, so great and precious a blessing it is, that God never imparts it to any fraudulent Montebanks, nor to tyrants, nor to any impure, lazy envious persons, nor to the effeminate and idle, nor to gluttons, nor usurers, nor to any worshippers of Mammon: But in all Ages, the pious, the charitable, the liberal, the meek, the patient, and indefatigable spirit, who was a diligent observer and admirer of his works, found it out. This truth is elegantly sung and expressly taught by that famous Philosopher and Poet, the excellent Augurellus.

The greedy cheat with impure hands may not
Attempt this Art, nor is it ever got, by the unlearned and rude: The villains mind
To lust and softness given, it strikes stark blind,
So the slym wandering Traitor and co. And shortly after.
But the sage, pious Man, who still adores
And loves his Maker, and his love implores
Whoever joys to search the Secret cause.
And series of his works, their love and laws,
Let Him draw near, and joining will with strength,
Study this Art in all her Depth and Length;
Then grave experience shall his consort be
Skilled in large Nature's inmost mystery.
The knots and doubts his busy course and cares
Will oft destruct, till time the truth declares,
And stable Patience (though all Trials past)
Brings the glad end and long hoped for, at last.

Give ear all you Medicasters, who hate and persecute this divine science; give ear, I say, and tell me with what conscience of honest confidence can you profess yourselves to be physicians, seeing that all Physick or Medicines are, without Chymistry, imperfect? Without that Chymistry, I say, which out of the manifested Light of Nature has its invincible grounds and canons laid down in this little book. This is the only Art, which (by supplying us, out of the Light of Nature, with convenient means and particular natures to separate the impure from the pure) will teach us first how to heal all diseases of the Macrocosmical substances, and afterwards by examples and experiments deducted from those exterior cures, will show us the right and infallible cure of all diseases in our own bodies.

He that knows not how to heal and purge metals, how can he restore the decayed or weakened radical Balsom in Man and excite it by comfortable and concordant Medicines to perform perfectly all his appointed functions, which must necessarily be put into action, before any disease can be expelled? He that knows not what that is in Antimony, which purges Gold, how can he come by an effectual and wholesome Medicine, that will purge and out those extraneous peccant causes and humors that afflict and destroy the body of Man?

He that knows not how to fix Arsenic, to take away the corrosive nature of sublimate, to coagulate sulphureous spirits, and by a convenient specifical Medicine to break and analyze stones in the greater world, will never in the body of Man allay and tame the Arsenical spirits of the Microcosmic Slat, nor take quite away the venomous indisposition of the Sulphur, nor dissolve the Stone in the bladder, and drive it out being dissolved. It is a noble safe and pious course we examine and try the force and virtues of Medicines upon the Microcosmical substances, before we apply them to our fellow creatures, and the rare fabric of Man.

This was the very consideration that moved the Ancients, who were true Philosophers, to a careful and effectual study of true Chymistry, the only genuine Philosophical Science, that by imitating Hermes, the Father and the Prince of all true and loyal Philosophers, they might find out most effectual and proper Medicines against all griefs and diseases, especially that glorious and supreme natural remedy, which is termed the Universal one, and is really without deception or exception (unless the finger of God oppose it) the most sure antidote of all diseases: For the obtaining of which sovereign Medicine, because this my treatise of Generation is no mean help. I would have it no longer concealed from the ingenious Lovers of this Art, but resolved to expose it to the Publick view, that the enemies of the truth may see and know, that our Science is grounded upon, and proceeded from the clear Light of Nature, and that all the Sons of Art may be more and more encouraged to a studious enquiry and a laborious search after the truth. If they benefit anything by this book, let them give God the glory, and lend me what further assistance they shall think fit to communicate.

Whatever it is, unto you, most noble and prudent Sir, my intimate Friend and my kinsman, I humbly do dedicate it; that you may see how willing I am to requite, in some measure, those numerous favours, which from the first day I entered upon this study, you have cheerfully conferred upon me, to this very hour. Therefore, I must entreat you to accept of this small Renumeration with your usual good will and benignity, still favorable to my endeavors, and to defend me from the calumnies and envy of the malicious, who from all parts set upon me and do defame my studies. This undeserved malignity I suffer under, will require your permanent favors and affection: And I do here solemnly promise, that I will never (God willing) do anything that shall tend to the violation of so sacred a friendship, and shall daily endeavor that we may be more and more endeared and closer united, which the only wise and good God mercifully grant, Amen! Farewell, most noble Sir, and as really do so continue still to further the studies of Your

Henry Nollius.

THE AUTHOR'S PREFACE TO HIS TREATISEOFGENERA TION

Being to write of the generation of natural things, I must ingenuously confess, that I learned it not in the books of the Athenian Sophisters (he means the Schoolmen, and the followers of Aristotle; this term he borrowed from Paracelsus, for he first called them so, and writing his Mysterium Magnum, entitled it, Philosophy for the Athenians, for Aristotle's school was at Athens), but by the true Light of Nature: Neither will I borrow any thing from them, or their books, and convert it in this discourse, like a Plagiary, to my own use or Glory; for the truth is not to be found in their books, but most gross ignorance and errors, grounded upon and supported by the vain men, which opinions the credulous people esteem and cry up as the utmost bounds and Non Ultra of all wisdom and perfection. As men are killed by fighting, so truth is lost by disputing; for while they only dispute and wrangle about Nature, every one of them in particular, and all of them in general are so filled and swollen up with a testy intolerable Pride and self worship, that each of them arrogating a kind of infallibility to his own Chimera's or monstrous conceits, does with all might and main labor to refute and demolish the airy castle and fond imaginations of the other, and by this ridiculous continued feud, they wander from the Bath and fundamentals of true knowledge, entangling themselves and too credulous posterity in an inextricable Labyrinth of quarrels and Errors, fortified with fictitious and groundless Principles never reduced to practice or trial, but merely suppose and implicitly believed, so that he would get out of this spacious and wearisome wilderness, cannot do it without much difficulty and laboriousness, and shall not do it without their general envy and opposition. Leaving therefore these lewd contenders and their verbosity, let us, the divine mercy assisting us, go directly to the house of wisdom by the Light of Nature, that by the simple and peaceable contemplation of the creatures, and her operations in them, we may truly discover and describe unto others the perfect manner of Generation, and so come not only to the certain knowledge of ourselves, but learn also how to produce and prepare out of perfect bodies and substance such a Medicine or Medicines as will innoxiously and faithfully cure all diseases that are incident t our own frail bodies: For as Men, Corn and Herbs are, every one of them, generated and born out of their own Specific Seed, so or in the same manner is the true Medicine of the Ancients (than which there cannot be a better) generated and prepared out of the most perfect bodies and essence. Look not therefore with careless and transient eyes upon what is offered thee in this book, but know and be assured that this Doctrine is the most profitable and advantageous for thee, by whose Light and guidance thou will be most prosperously led to the true knowledge of the Secret generation of all Animals, Vegetables, and Minerals, and to the finding out of that rich and rare Medicine which perfectly cures all imperfect Metals.

OfTheGenera tionOfNa turalThings

To begin then: You are to know in the first place, that generation is two fold, first Ordinary and second Extraordinary. Extraordinary generation is that by which an unlike thing is generated out of dung and putrefaction by the sun. This generation is termed in the schools equivocal. The Ordinary is that by which a like thing begets his like, as when a man begets a manchild, and a lion begets a lion. This in the schools is termed univocal. This generation with the method and the means I shall include in these ten following Aphorisms or propositions.

1

Everything generated or begotten is generated and born of his own specific seed (1) and in his proper (2) matrix.

The Commentary or Illustration.

(1) Seed is a spiritual or subtile body, out of which the included spirits, by attraction of nutriment to it, forms and produces, in his proper matrix, a living body, endued with the like prolific and multiplicable seed. This very spirit is by some Philosophers termed seed, and the body in which it resides they call sperm. But while we agree about the matter I shall not quarrel about words. This seminal spirit is the most subtile essence of the seed, exalted by Nature out of some perfect body and containing in it, after the most eminent and perfect manner, all the virtues and faculties of the said body, and in a seminific power besides, which enables it, in its own species, to propagate and multiply its own body.

(2) No kind of seed is of any virtue or effect, unless its be placed by Nature, or by Art, in its proper matrix (See Apor. VIII). That matrix is only proper and fostering which is naturally agreeable and ordained for the seed, according to its particular species and regimen. Therefore mineral seeds require a mineral matrix, vegetable seeds a vegetable, and animal seeds an animal matrix.

The matrix of mineral seeds are subterraneous mines, the earth is the matrix of vegetables and the female womb is the matrix of animal seeds.

2

Before any perfect thing can be generated the seed mus necessarily putrefy and tehn be nourished:

Commentary

Believe our Savior John XII, 22, "Verily, verily I say unto you, except a corn of wheat fall into the ground and die, it abides alone; bit if it die it bringeth forth much fruit".

"Nothing can be animated and born unless it first suffer corruption, putrefaction and mortification", says Raymond Lully in his Testament, see Rosar. Philo., page 254.

Therefore say Paramenides, unless the body be dissolve and broken and putrefied and suffer a change in its substantial substance, that secret central virtue cannot be extracted nor be at liberty to mix with another body.

3

The seed putrefies when a (1) salt of the same nature with it, dissolved in a convenient (2) liquor, does by the assistance of a gentle heat (3) penetrate, analyze and rarify the substance of the seed, that the included spirit may, out of its subject matter, form a convenient (4) habitation or body for itself, in which it may perform the offices of natural generation and seminal multiplication.

Commentary

(1) Therefore every mineral seed requires to its purification a mineral salt and liquor; which is common water impregnated with saltpeter; and animal seeds require an animal salt and liquor, which is the female menstruum impregnated with the salt of the animal matrix. By this doctrine a passage of the most acute Philosopher Basil Valentine in his treatise of the world's great mystery, is easily understood. The words are these: "Metals and minerals must be dissolved and reduced again to their first matter by minerals, but in doing this you must in every sort of mineral consider the species or kind; for every kind mixes only with his own kind, and so yields his seed, unless you will have a monster. The virtues and propension of every seed is to join and mix itself with every thing that is within its own order or latitude; for no seed naturally applies to anything that is Extra Regnum Suum; therefore in any ordinary and lawful generation, that one like may beget another, man applies to woman, the lion to the lioness", etc.

(2) Without the humour of water (says Basil Valentine, in his eighth key), true putrefaction can never be performed: For humours or liquors are the true mediums by which salt does by his dissolving and searching nature enter into and open the most intricate recesses of the seed; for when this humour or liquor is by a due degree of heat rarified and provoked, then also is the salt in it attenuated and rendered fit to pass into and open the most compacted body of the seed, and there stirs up and excites to vegetation a spirit of salt that is the like and the same with itself, which before lay hid and inactive.

(3) A spirit that is at liberty will easily and quickly free another spirit of the same nature that is bound up and restrained. This is done first by reason of that activity and generability which the free spirit is imbued with, secondly by reason of the harmony, likeness and love betwixt them: This correlation is the cause that the exterior free spirit makes way into and joins with that spirit of salt included in the seed, and so does with more ease work upon him and excite him, for, as the proverb has it, like will easily go to like, and their unity is most intimate. Now you must know that very spirit, when loose and floating in liquid bodies or liquors, is at liberty in this state, by the mediation of heat, it does (like a lodestone) attract to it the spirit that is under restraint, opening and dissolving the body which holds it in; and the restrained spirit itself (like a sensible prisoner) labours for life by conspiring and striving to be in action and a full communion with the other. The free spirit by his sudden and subtile accession still exciting and strengthening him, and by this means so provokes him to action, as fire, does enkindle fire so that the body holding it must necessarily suffer a change and calcification, and comes to be putrefied by its own included spirit, whose operation before was obstructed and kept under; for the included spirit having acquired liberty and a power to be in action from the other, strives to get out and enlarge itself, and to that end breaks and destroys its first body and procures another new one. So the spirit of salt of the earth, when it is dissolved in the unmixed humour of that element (since every salt melts in its own liquor) is then at liberty; for every salt when it is once dissolved in its own liquor becomes active. Hence it is that a corn of wheat (in whose body, as if under lock and key, the spirit of vegetable salt is bound up and fettered) as soon as it is cast into the ground, is by the free spirit of the salt of the earth penetrated and opened, that the salt which lies dissolved or loose in that liquor or inmixed humour may excite the vegetable spirit in the corn of wheat to action and vegetation, which spirit being thus set at liberty does presently, by putrefaction of the corn or grain, produce in the wheat's proper matrix the substance of the root (which is a new body) by whose mediation and deference the earth must afterwards (the spirit attracting it)communicate nutriment to the blade and the rest of this vegetable as it grows up and increases. You must observe here that this salt which conduces to the solution and opening of bodies is sometimes weak, sometimes strong. If it be weak you must strengthen it with a salt that is of the same nature and property with the seed; and the liquor which has the weak salt in it must be impregnated with it; that the solution may be more effectual and more convenient for nature in the operations. Let us consider the generation of wheat. There is in rainwater a volatile salt by solution made in the earth; but when that salt, by reason of the earth's over dryness, is not sufficient to cause a perfect and fruitful solution of the seed corn, then does the husbandman strengthen and manure his ground with muck and dung in which there is a salt of the same nature with the seed; so that when the rain descends and mixes itself with the compost or mould, there proceeds from the muck and the ground a nitrosulphureous salt which the inmixed humour of the earth imbibes or takes in, and being strengthened by it opens the most compacted and firmest seeds, whence comes a fruitful and joyful harvest. If thou desire to see the secrets of Nature now open thine eyes.

(4) Seeing that the seminal virtue lurks in the most intricate recesses of the seed, and consist in the most subtile portion of the sulphureous salt, it is most clear that it cannot be exalted and multiplied but in an humour that is most eminently subtile and pure: but because the seed sown does not at the first or presently take in that subtile humour out of those places which supply it with nutriment. Therefore Nature does, before all things, take care first to produce and form those vessels in which that humour, taken afterwards out of the elements, is digested, rarified and most accurately purged, that out of the whole body when formed and perfected, she may contribute and produce the most pure seminal essence, for the conservation and the multiplication of that species which yields it; for which very reason provident Nature does, by the intervening of putrefaction, out of the seed sof herbs form first the roots, and out of the roots she does afterwards shoot forth the blade, driving it, in the growth, into several sections or joints. That the humour taken out of the soil in which the seed is sown may, at the first in the root and afterwards in the herb (when grown up and flourishing) be more and more digested, and drive the seminal virtue (through all the vessels and joints) from the very root to the uppermost top branches, where, in a matrix purposely formed for the reception of this seminal matter, a most perfect seed, and fit for the propagation of the same species, is (by the aid of the Sun heat maturing it) found and gathered. But it happens often times (and this you are concerned to know) that though Nature forms always these vessels and vehicular of the seminal progression, yet those bodies which are thus furnished, do not always yield seed; and this comes to pass because, in those bodies, the pores through which the spermatic virtue should be promoted and driven into their superficies and upper parts, are (before the seed is stirred, or can be produced) stopped up by external colds; or else by the predominant virtue of their innate fixed salt are so bound up and obstructed that the seed either cannot come to any effectual maturity and perfection, or else is wholly suppressed and shut up. An example of this we may manifestly see in the orange trees, which grow indeed in this climate as well as other plants, but in this cold region yield no fruits: Whereas in Italy and other places, which are their natural soil, they both yield and bring forth fruit to perfection. In the like manner gold and other metals which come to our hands can make no emission of their included seed, because their pores are, by the vigor and excellency of their innate fixed salt, so bound and shut up that they are wholly restrained from the effusion of seed; so that the seminal virtue in them is not at liberty to act and come forth; for which very reason the Philosophers who knew this and were willing to assist Nature, did with most happy success reduce Gold and the other metals into their first matter, that by this course they might open their pores, which by the super-eminent vigor and power of the innate fixed salt were shut up and locked, and so bring the metals to that pass and condition in which they might, with a marvelous increase and to their great benefit, yield seed and propagate: Not otherwise then when the orange trees in the Maurice garden at Cacels are all winter long cherished with an external artificial heat, which makes them put forth and bring their fruits to maturity. He that hath ears to hear let him hear.

4

The humour or liquor which serves for putrefaction must be proportionable to that body which is to be putrefied.

Commentary

The humour must then be proportioned both for quantity and receptivity. The humour is proportioned for quantity when so much of it is taken in by the body as is sufficient for its subtilisation. It is proportioned for receptivity or the manner of reception, when the humour is not suddenly and at once, but gently and by degrees, or by little and little, taken in and drunk up by the body or seed: For a sudden imbibation of the humour cannot so conveniently vivify the seed, but causes by its sudden and unequal penetration, that some parts of the body or seed are insufficiently opened or dissolved; hence it happens that Darnel does sometimes come up instead of corn. Therefore the Philosophers advise the sons of this science to irrigate, or moisten our earth by long delay and a frequent and wearisome attrition.

5

The heat which promotes this putrefaction must be so mild and temperate that the liquor in which the resolving salt lies may remain still in and about the matter, and not be laved or evaporated from it.

Commentary

This must be done for two reasons: first, because the body putrefying must receive life in this liquor: second, because such a gentle heat dissolves the salt in the liquor without violence and disperses it into the matter after a natural manner that the body may now conveniently putrefy; but if the liquor were agitated by an excessive heat the matter in it would be destroyed or spoiled so that it could neither be animated nor receive such a putrefaction as is convenient for it, and therefore nothing (in this case) could be generated out of the matter. Listen to this Pamphilius! Thou that aims at the universal medicine.

6

The body putrefying must not be removed out of the matrix in which the putrefaction was begun until that which is intended be fully perfected.

Commentary

Therefore when we would out of our grain of corn get a whole ear we leave it in the earth until the appointed time of harvest, and then we find the ear ripe and carry it home. Seeds (says Avicen) should not be gathered until the harvest comes.

7

The more pure the matrix is, the thing generated is by so much the more perfect and sound.

Commentary

For the pure matrix (says Leschus) will yield pure fruit. Now the more pure any thing is it is so much the more perfect and durable in its kind: On the contrary the impure, it is so much the more imperfect and frail. Therefore an impure matrix, because it yields impure fruit, must necessarily also produce it weak, impermanent, and useless.

Which inconvenience being found in everything, wise men willing to assist nature, attempted to putrefy and heal the impure matrix, wherever they found it.

From these attempts spring a most wise and sure experience, which taught them all impurities and extraneous natures which hindered the generation or fostering of the birth in the matrix were either by a natural or else by an artificial assistance to be removed and taken away.

Now, when for the separation of subtile delitiscent impurities, or the removal of any weakness, Nature requires any help, this must be done by a judicious and discerning knowledge: But after separation, when these impurities are once excluded from the matrix and are only a hindrance to generation by their incumbrance and abode in place, then there is only required a manual operation as volution or ejection. We find a plain demonstration of this in the art of tillage or husbandry, where the infirm salt of the earth is by the sulphurous fat salt of the dung assisted and strengthened; but the stones and thistles which lie separated from the matrix and hinder its fertility only by their weight and incumbrance are, by mere handy work cast out and rooted up, that the matrix of the corn thus dressed may become and be called a fruitful field.

The same method do Philosophers use in their magistry and practice; for they do first purge their field or matrix, then they enrich or strengthen it with the Sulphur of nature: And lastly, cast in their seed, that it may be vivified and multiplied, and be turned into a most noble and effectual medicine.

8

That matrix is only convenient and adapted to generation which permits an easy entrance to the seed.

Commentary

This is to say, which receives it with ease and is no hindrance by its hardness or closeness to the entrance of the seed. Here you must know that when the matrix, by reason of hardness, is grown callous and impenetrable, it is then opened and rendered porous again by frequent agitation that it may be fitted for the conception of seed. So the husbandman do plough up first, then mattocks and afterwards harrow their green sward or untilled lands and beat every clod asunder, that by this rarefaction and dissolution, the earth may take and easily receive in the seed, and put it forth again with increase.

If thou desire to come by the secrets of God, and to use them rightly to his glory and the good of thy neighbor, then do thou, in this Philosophic task set before thine eyes the laborious and patient husbandman, and be sure to imitate him, then will God, without doubt, favor thy righteous attempts, and give that into thy possession which will perfectly satisfy all the longings of thy heart.

9

Out of that Body which is either corrupted or destroyed by strange or extraneous natures; or whose spermatic vessels are by some violence maimed or cut off no seed can be had.

Commentary

It will be a very vain and unprofitable attempt for any to hope for issue or healthful seed by a man whose body and radical balsam is deprived or dried up by an excess of aromatic wines or hot water, or by some contagious disease. Eunuchs, because their genitals are cut off, cannot propagate their own species. Let the Sons of the Science know (says the most ingenious Leschus) that it is very fruitless work to look for that in dry twigs and lopped branches which can never be found but in the green and living.

10

That body which is preserved or sustains by one simple kind of nutriment is far more perfect and durable and yields more sound and perfect seeds than that which is nourished with many different kinds of nutriment.

Commentary

For the nearer anything is to unity it is so much the more durable; for in unity there is no division or discord, which is the cause of corruption, and where no corruption is there is a permanent integrity and conservation. Therefore that which is nearest to unity must needs keep better and endure longer than that which is more remote. Because there is in the one less discord and more durable anything is the seed it yields is by so much the more perfect and permanent.

[The English edition of this work extends only thus far. The five following chapters have never been published in English.]

11

How the Fountain of the Wise Men Becomes Lead

(1) Nature uses nothing else for the generating of lead but our fountain, that is our mercuries.

(2) Because she takes the full moisture of all the Elements, mixed with the heavenly vivifying Spirit of Light, and compound the same with all sort s of heterogenial, terrestrial and sulphureous moistures, and including them in the cavities of the earth, bakes them and digests the matter a long time.

(3) When all is well united by purification or putrefaction, then she continues to bake it without separating the impure, until all is become a black glittering and heavy earth, out of which afterwards, with a small fire, lead is melted.

(4) But his ore of lead is not the matter of the Stone of the Wise Men with which they transmute imperfect metals into Gold and Silver. Common lead has no such perfection that out of it should be prepared the white and red sulphur of the Wise Men, for in lead they are very raw and imperfect, which imperfection cannot be established but by the tincture itself.

(5) Our Stone is prepared out of our fountain only, which differs very much from common lead, for our mercury is not common lead but the Father thereof.

(6) And although our fountain or mercury often is called lead, yet the Wise Men always understood thereby our fountain out of which alone our elixir is prepared; because our Saturn or fountain, when it has dissolved its magnesia or earth out of which it issued, and is again coagulated together by a small fire, becomes a black heavy earth, which compound is then called the lead of the Wise Men.

(7) He that can make the lead unto him the whole Art is open, for in it lies hid the Gold and Silver of the Wise Men; that is the white and red sulphur tinging all imperfect metals either into Gold or Silver.

(8) Of this lead or Saturn the poets have written much, telling us that Saturn devours all his children, etc. Note this. His Sulphur consumes all that is hid in the matter enclosed in its belly, digests and concocts it to its ripeness.

(9) But Jupiter, observing this, with sharp scythe cuts off the stones of his father Saturn and throws them into the sea, because the white sulphur, which in the operation appears after blackness, abolishes by his piercing power, which is here called the scythe, the strong power of the black sulphur called Saturn and throws the same into the sea. That black sulphur comes to be dissolved and changed into a sea, out of which the fair Venus is generated which is the green color.

(10) Saturn endeavors to devour Jupiter or the white sulphur, but instead of him he swallows a stone which was laid before him, which he spews up again upon the mount of Helicon. There the same was erected as a monument for mortals.

(11) Also our Saturn endeavors to devour the white color that appears after blackness, but the same is changed into a stone. For though Saturn devours the stone yet by continual concoction it is cast up again.

(12) Our thus dissolved matter is coagulated into the stone of the Wise men, which isto dissolved again, and in this manner Saturn always devours a stone instead of Jupiter, which he spews up upon Helicon, until at length it becomes our blessed Stone which is dedicated to Wisdom.

(13) Out of this our Jupiter and Latona are born Apollo and Diana. This is the last and perfect coction, in which the white and red sulphurs, that is Apollo and Diana, acquire their plusquam perfection.

(14) Hence we see that our Saturn or lead is the father of all the gods, for from himcome all the metals.

12

How the Fountain of the Wise Men becomes Quicksilver

Commentary

(1) Between our fountain and common quicksilver there is so great a sympathy. Yea such an one that by many they are counted to be but one thing. But they err, because our fountain is the Father of quicksilver and therefore differs much from common quicksilver.

(2) Our fountain generates and makes alive all things. Common quicksilver destroys, corrupts and kills all.

(3) Our fountain is fiery and hot. Common mercury is moist and cold.

(4) Our fountain is changed by a small distillation into a spirit a fixed body, but common mercury is a mere spirit and cannot be changed into a watery spirit, but rises corporeally without alteration.

(5)The extracted spirit of our fountain is fiery, sharp, penetrating and subtile, so that it can dissolve and kill all metals; but the common quicksilver cannot be made into a spirit, neither can it dissolve and kill metals: It hides them in its belly, but by a small fire it leaves them again unchanged.

(6) Our Fountain dissolves, coagulates, and makes itself, without addition of any thing: None of which can common mercury do, neither can it be coagulated without addition of other species.

(7) Our fountain has within it a fixed salt white and red. Yea it is all salt and issues out of a saltish cavity; but the common mercury is nothing but a running metal, and if we will make salt out of it we must putrefy and kill it.

(8) Our fountain is potentially Gold and Silver, which by coction may be got out of it, which cannot be got out of common quicksilver.

(9) Our fountain becomes by mere coction, without and addition, the Elixir of the Wise Men, but this cannot be expected of common mercury.

(10) In our fountain are all metals potentially; because it is the seed out of which the common metals, yea quicksilver itself grows, which cannot be said of common quicksilver.

(11) Our fountain in earth all sorts of stones, noble and ignoble, which common mercury cannot do.

(12) Nature mixes earth with our fountain a very subtile and clean body, and includes them in the cavities of the earth, bakes and digests it like other metals until it becomes a dark, red, glittering earth, which is called the mineral or natural cinnabar, which is distilled by a small fire into running quicksilver.

(13) Yea there are vapours sublimed out of the mercurial mineral or ore of cinnabar, which in cold places run together again and become mercury.

(14) Thus in many places mercury is found upon the superficies of the earth which have been sublimed out of its hidden minera, and by the coldness of the night and of the heavenly dew gathered together and made running.

13

How Our Fountain becomes known or manifested to the Wise Men.

Commentary

(1) Our fountain must be prepared out of two saline substances, yet of one root, otherwise it is impossible that it pass or be acknowledged for ours.

(2) These two slain substances yield by a small fire a very fiery spirit which has innumerable names.

(3) When this spirit is drawn off from them they remain as dead earth behind, because they have lost their spirit by distillation.

(4) But if we give the dead earth its spirit again it becomes, by a soft fire, dissolved again and a blood red liquor, which by coction becomes redder and redder, then black, and at last thick and fat.

(5) The dead earth, before it is joined again with its spirit has also many names from the Wise Men, as may be seen in their writings.

(6) When this spirit by due coction is once united with its body they can never be separated again.

(7) Because by continued decoction they become fixt and abiding in the fire, and although they flow in the fire yet they fume not away.

(8) Thus our matter has a twofold name, yet it comes from one root.

(9) It is mineral and Nature has given it a mineral form, but left the same imperfect: it flows easily: It is compounded of volatile and fixed, and when they are united they purify, and then they become perfect.

(10) In this operation they become all sorts of colors as black, white, red. After redness they change no more.

(11) This matter after having received perfect whiteness, perfect redness and fixation, tinges all imperfect metals into the best Silver and Gold.

(12) By this time our fountain is made manifest, unto which we must add that the volatile part thereof is of a very sour taste, penetrating nature, and sharp quality.

14

Whether Our Fountain to Come to its Perfection Stands in Need of Common Gold and Silver?

Commentary

(1) Our Fountain cannot come to its perfection without Gold and Silver, but this Sub and Moon are not common Su and Moon, but something else not strange to our Fountain neither against it.

(2) Because that Su and Moon which contributes to the perfection of our fountain and is first part thereof, of a double nature, white and red, the white is called Silver and the red Gold.

(3) Hence it appears to be very true our fountain cannot be brought to perfection without Silver and Gold, for Gold and Silver are the fixt and permanent part thereof, which can, shall and must fix the volatile.

(4) It is of that of which is sung: "By Art dissolve the fixt and after let it fly; And fix the Volatile that not it rise high".

(5) It is the Gold which must be dissolved and changed into a spirit by its own spirit.

(6) We cannot say so of common Gold, for where must we get the spirit of common Sol and with the same dissolve it and change it into a spirit. This is also to be understood of common Silver.

(7) Therefore when we speak of Gold and Silver we always understand which are in our fountain and are innate in it.

(8) The spirit of the heavenly sun, when untied with the fat moisture of the elements, by his heat fixes and coagulates, and produces a peculiar salt which appropriates to itself the virtues and qualities of the heavenly light and strives to become like its father. Hence the Wise Men have Gold, whereas in truth it is salt and has the nature of salt.

(9) And yet it is but one and not a twofold salt, as if one should be Sol and the other Luna: No, it is only one salt, called either Sol or Luna after a different manner.

(10) And yet it is but one and a twofold salt, as if one should be Sol and the other Luna: No, it is only one salt, called either Sol or Luna after a different manner.

(11) When our salt has acquired the highest whiteness then we call it Luna, but when it comes to the highest redness then we call it Sol. Our fountain cannot subsist without this Sol or Luna, and what we say cannot be applied to common Sol and Luna.

(12) And although the Wise Men want some common Gold in the fermentation of their Stone, that the same may be determined to transmute imperfect metals into Sol, it does not therefore follow that common Sol should make perfect our Stone.

(13) On the contrary our Stone rather makes perfect common Sol and Luna, because the most perfect Sol is imperfect and unfruitful without our Stone. But when it comes to be united to our Stone it becomes alive and fruitful and can communicate part of its perfection to other metals.

(14) Many busy themselves in endeavors to dissolve common Gold and bring it into a true essence but in vain. It is a labour not worth once thinking on.

(15) There is another solution which is true and natural, which is performed by itself, because the solvent and that which is to be dissolved in it are both of one substance. Therefore are they radically dissolved.

(16) We must look after this solution and not the common, because our solvent, our Sol, and our Luna, although they seem to be together yet are but one thing and are in one substance.

(17) This a fool cannot understand: As soon as he hears this he falls into errors, not only in what concerns the preparation of the matter but also in the administration of the fire, making of the oven, making of the furnace, closing the vessels and the determination of the weight.

(18) The powerful virtue and operation of the light in our matter is our weight. He that does not know and understand this must certainly err.

15

How Much Our Fountain wants of its Gold and Silver to come to its Perfection

Commentary

(1) Nature has no weight in the generation of metals, because it has but one only matter wherein it works.

(2) But in making our fountain every one is admonished to take of the weight because our fountain consists of two matters, one being the male, the other the female, in whose conjunction we must needs trouble ourselves about the weight. In joining make and female together this our fountain is borne.

(3) But every weight will not serve in this work, but only that which has its due determination.

(4) Know therefore that equal parts of both these matters are to be taken in the celebration of our first marriage, but in the second marriage in which the volatile is joined with the fixed the weight must be otherwise considered.

(5) For the fixed part must be dissolved by the volatile and turned into water: Hence there must be more of the volatile than of the fixt in this solution and conjunction.

(6) Some take ten parts of the volatile tone part of the fixt, some seven, some but three. It suffices that so much of the volatile water be taken as the solution of the fixt part requires.

(7) Much water dissolves quickly, but then the coagulation which follows takes the longer; on which the ignorant, not knowing the nature of this work, fall into desperation when they perceive that the work does not coagulate in due time.

(8) I have taken much water, but then after dissolution the superfluous is abstracted again, and God has blessed my work richly.

(9) There is yet another way to be used in the multiplication to moisten the white and the red work, which is done by our highly rectified fountain; and here you must be very cautious. For the white you must only pour the thickness of a paper upon it, which must be often repeated until the Stone is perfectly satiated and it becomes white and red.

(10) In this operation Art does not follow Nature, for Art stands in need of a certain weight but Nature is her own weight, for she takes as much as is necessary and thrusts away the rest, reserving it for other uses. Nature has nothing useless or superfluous, for what is not good for this is good for another thing.

(11) Know for a conclusion tat you need take care for nothing but to acquire our fountain (unto which will not only serve you this Treatise, but also my other treatise entitled, *The Rules of Wisdom and Chemistry* with my third one called *Sanguis Naturae* which will give you sufficiently, yea abundant instruction and expositions) because this fountain comprehends the whole Philosophical work, makes the same and corrects all errors, if perhaps committed. Besides this fountain is to be highly esteemed, because we want neither fire nor furnaces nor vessel, for our fountain is all these if you understand it right.

(12) Hast thou obtained this fountain then thou hast whole Nature in thy power. Thou lacking nothing, but have all things that thou desire already in thy hand, for which praise Jehovah!

Table des matières